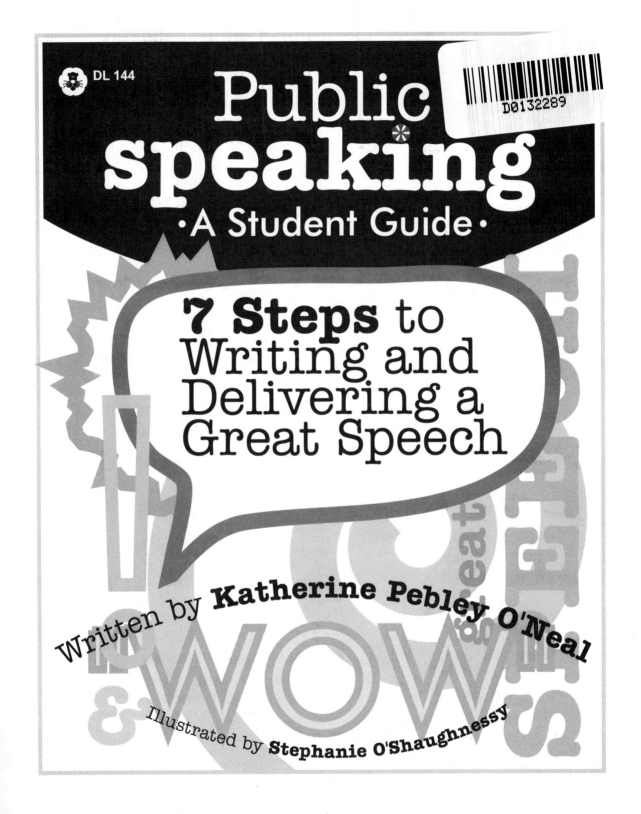

DL 144

Public speaking
·A Student Guide·

7 Steps to Writing and Delivering a Great Speech

Written by **Katherine Pebley O'Neal**

Illustrated by **Stephanie O'Shaughnessy**

ISBN 1-883055-52-0

For more information about Dandy Lion products, visit our website
www.dandylionbooks.com

Contents • • • • • • • • • • • • •

Introduction

Why Give a Great Oral Report? • • • • • •

In classroom 5A, Bobby is reading his report on Idaho from a sheet of note paper. He never looks at the class. His voice is too low for the kids in the back row to hear. Three kids are gazing out the window, two others are reading novels, and the teacher's eyelids are drooping. Afterwards, nobody remembers anything about Idaho, not even Bobby.

* * * * * * * *

Meanwhile, in room 5B, you are presenting your own report about Idaho. Your colorful flip charts illustrate each of your major points and they help you to remember what to say without having to read it. You hand out maps of the United States with Idaho circled in gold. As you come to the end of your talk, you serve a few Idaho potato chips to each of your classmates. Suddenly, Idaho is everyone's favorite state.

Why should you bother to give a great oral report? Why has your teacher assigned one, anyway? Some of the reasons for learning how to make effective oral reports are:

✳ Oral reports are an excellent way to get lots of information to the whole class.

✳ When you study something and then teach or tell about it to someone else, you understand it even better yourself.

✳ Giving a great oral report will boost your self-esteem and make you feel proud.

✳ Public speaking is a skill you will use throughout your life.

✳ It's fun!

In this book you will learn how to organize your information into a presentation that will interest and amaze your classmates. You will discover exciting ways to start your speech, clever ways to end your speech, and lots of intelligent techniques to use in the middle to keep your audience attentive. You will discover tricks to keep you from feeling nervous, and special, easy ways to remember what you want to say. Using your new skills, you will be entertaining, informative and confident.

Chapter 1

Get Organized • • • • • • • • • • • • • • • • • •

A great oral report is full of good information. It gets people's attention with something they can easily relate to, it holds their interest, and it gives them new knowledge. Your talk will be fun to give and interesting to listen to if you pack it with exciting information. Here's how to get started.

✏️ Choose your topic

First, choose a topic that interests you. The purpose of giving a report is to share information with your class. If you like your topic, planning your report will be more fun.

Next, make sure your topic is the right size. If you choose a huge topic, like "The Amazing Human Body," your talk could go on for hours or even days. Narrow your topic down to one aspect that interests you, like "The Amazing Human Nose." Get your topic approved by your teacher.

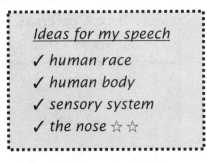

Ideas for my speech
✓ *human race*
✓ *human body*
✓ *sensory system*
✓ *the nose* ☆ ☆

Know what you are trying to accomplish with your presentation. Are you trying to educate, convince, entertain, or demonstrate? Once you know what your goal is, everything you say should be directed toward meeting that goal.

"My goal is to educate you about all the ways your nose helps you sense the world around you."

"By the end of my speech, everyone will be able to identify four birds that live in our area."

"By the time I finish talking, you will be convinced that James Dogood is the best candidate for mayor."

Make an outline

If your teacher gives you requirements for the information you need to include in your speech, use that list as a basic outline. Gather the required information first. You can add extra details later.

If you have a topic but no specific outline to follow, general reference books can give you a good overall picture of your topic. Reference books to check include an encyclopedia, almanac, atlas, and dictionary.

Use these books to make a list of important things you want to tell the class, and this will be your rough outline. Reference books can help you decide whether your topic is too small to find enough information or too big for one report. You can also get clues about where else to look for information.

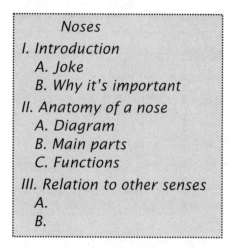

Noses
I. Introduction
  A. Joke
  B. Why it's important
II. Anatomy of a nose
  A. Diagram
  B. Main parts
  C. Functions
III. Relation to other senses
  A.
  B.

✎ Find other sources of information

Now that you have a plan, go to the library. Use your outline to help you find books on your topic. Nonfiction books are arranged by subject in the library, so if you look up your topic on the library computer, it will list all the books on that topic and they will most likely be shelved together. For "The Amazing Human Nose," you could use the key words nose, nostril, olfactory or smell to find related books. Remember, the librarian would love to help you.

Don't forget other sources of information. Museums, zoos, and art galleries have lots of information. The Internet is full of facts. Interviewing real people can give you a firsthand perspective. If your topic has information that changes, get the most up-to-date information from current newspapers, periodicals and almanacs.

✎ Take Notes

The easy way to take notes is to use note cards. You will need an adequate supply of cards so you can record all the information you find. The first card should list all your sources, with the author and publication data, like this:

> 1. _The World's Largest Noses_ by J. Honker, Tissue Publications, Chicago, 2000.
> 2. _The Guinness Book of World Records, 1999_, Guinness Publishing Ltd., Bantam Books, New York, 1999.

Then skim or read through your reference material. Whenever you find something you want to put in your report, write it in your own words on a new note card, with the source number and page at the top, like this:

> 2, p. 157
> The most famous nose belonged to Jimmy Durante, a Hollywood movie star in the 1930's.
>
> Nicknamed "Da Schnozz ," his nose was insured for $100,000.

JIMMY DURANTE

Write Your Rough Draft

When you have finished taking notes, it's time to put together your rough draft. The great thing about note cards is you can change their order until your information is organized in a way that flows smoothly and makes sense. Organizing and rewriting your notes into a report helps you to use your own words, too, so the report will be yours and not a copy of someone else's work.

The best way to start writing is to dig right in. This is only a rough draft. You are the author and you can change anything at any time. When you are happy with what you have written, read it out loud. Do you still like it? If so, it's time to turn it into an oral presentation that will impress your audience.

Chapter 2

Grab Their Attention ● ● ● ● ● ● ● ● ● ● ●

A great opening line will grab the attention of your audience. It will help them focus on your topic so they will listen and learn from what you have to say. There are several ways to get this attention.

Ask a question

"How many of you think you could smell the difference between cinnamon and garlic with your eyes closed?"

"How many of you have been on a roller coaster before?"

"Who knows the difference between an alligator and a crocodile?"

Questions like these will draw your classmates in and create interest for what you have to say next. Ask questions that can be answered with a show of hands so your classmates won't have to speak out.

🗨 Share a story

Stories capture interest and add a personal touch to your report. Keep them short and relevant to your topic.

"The summer before last my dad broke his nose water-skiing. He had to keep it packed with gauze for a month while it healed. During that time, he couldn't smell or taste. The human nose is amazing."

" I first got interested in whales when we were on a fishing trip and a whale surfaced very close to our boat. It was then I knew that these gentle giants were special animals."

🗨 Give an impressive fact

Giving a little-known or impressive fact or making a dramatic statement to open your talk will show that you're an expert on your subject. Then use the fact to move smoothly into your topic.

"Jimmy Durante, a movie star from the 1930's, not only had a nickname for his nose, he had it insured for $100,000. Most of the noses in this classroom aren't that famous, but they are pretty amazing, all the same."

" The blue whale, the largest creature on earth, is about 100 feet or 30 meters in length. This is just one of the impressive things about these marine mammals."

🗨 Use audience imagination

Ask your listeners to close their eyes and imagine something that you describe. Make the visualization short and something everyone can associate with.

"Close your eyes and think about walking through the forest. Imagine the green trees surrounding you. What smells do you sense?"

"Close you eyes and imagine you are in a roller coaster. You have just reached the top of the curve. Feel your stomach jump as you drop down, down, down, going faster and faster. The force you feel is called g force or gravitational force."

"Imagine walking into a pizza place at dinnertime. Spicy aromas surround you, savory sauce, melted cheese, warm crisp crust. Now open your eyes and raise your hands to tell me what you smelled with your amazing nose."

🗨 Tell a joke

Even a simple joke can set a light-hearted tone for you report. Make sure your joke is tasteful, relates to your topic, and can lead directly into the body of your speech.

> *"Which dogs are best for sending telegrams?*
> *Wire haired terriers. Today I am going to tell you about a breed of dogs called terriers."*

🗨 Pretend to answer a letter

Open an envelope and read an imaginary letter or question aloud. Then use your speech to answer the question. You can come back to the letter at the end to close your talk if you wish.

> *"John, from Arizona, writes, 'Why is the human nose so amazing?' Well, John, I can answer that question."*

🗨 Announce your objectives

Tell your audience what you hope to accomplish with this speech. This works best when your presentation needs to be no-nonsense and professional.

> *"Today I am going to prove to you that the human nose is truly amazing. By the end of my presentation, you will understand seven reasons why the human nose is essential in our lives."*

> *"I am going to explain how to make a hanging flower basket in five easy steps. By the time I finish, you will be able to create your own beautiful basket for your garden or patio."*

> *"I know everyone hates to spend their evenings doing homework, so I am going to give you five easy ways to get organized and finish your homework in less time."*

Chapter **3**

End With Style ·

Ending your presentation is easy. The best conclusions summarize or reinforce the main points of your talk. Good endings help your classmates remember what you said. A dramatic ending can even save an otherwise bland speech. Here are some ways to add pizazz to the ending of your speech.

◎ Provide a list

You can say the list or show it on a visual aid. The list should sum up the main points you made during your report in the order you made them.

> *"So remember:*
> *1. Noses are vital for both breathing and smelling.*
> *2. Nose parts include the nostril, the septum, and two nasal passages.*
> *3. Smell and taste are closely related. And,*
> *4. The human nose is truly amazing."*

◎ Give advice

Advice is something the audience can take with them to remember your speech. It also gives the listeners something to do with the information you have given them.

"So remember, take good care of your amazing nose!"

"When you go to the tide pools, you can admire all the fabulous sea life in the pools but don't take anything home with you."

◎ Be funny

Review the facts in your report to see if there is anything you can use to make up a funny closing line. Tell a humorous anecdote or just add an amusing last line. Remember, clever or silly is fine. It doesn't have to be hilarious.

"That just about covers the amazing human nose. So long, good-bye, smell you later!"

"And this ends your visit to the underwater world of whales. Time to surface and get ready for math."

◎ Ask for questions

"Now that I've told you about the amazing human nose, do you have any questions for me?"

I have given you enough basic information to start your own herb garden, but do you have any specific questions?"

Be prepared to answer questions before you decide to use this ending. Pause slightly before you answer each question. You should answer at least three questions, each from a different person, before saying that's all the time you have for answering questions.

◎ Make a rhyme

Rhyming is very effective if it includes some real information that you want your audience to remember about your topic. It doesn't have to be great poetry to be a memorable ending.

"So remember —
You can't smell a rose
without your nose,
And trying to taste
would be a waste."

◎ Give your audience a task

Audience participation will help your listeners feel important and help them remember your speech. The audience will enjoy taking part in your ending, and this can also be funny.

"Now, please turn to the person on your left and shake hands with the owner of an amazing human nose."

"On the piece of paper I gave you at the start of the speech quickly write down three facts about whales."

"Work with the person seated next to you to recall five products Mexico exports. Raise you hand when you have named five products."

◎ Ask for action

A call to action works best if your topic lends itself to action, like "Benefits of Recycling" or "Our Polluted Lakes." But other less serious topics can also call for action.

"I would like each of you to go home and tell your parents about their noses. Be sure they know just how amazing the human nose truly is."

"Now that you know what a good cause this is, I know that many of you will want to sign up for the walk-a-thon."

◎ Give a handout

Handouts give listeners something to take with them to remember your important information. Have the handouts copied and ready, within easy reach at the end of your talk. Make enough copies for everyone in the class, including your teacher.

"In conclusion, I am handing out a list of important nose facts."

"I am going to give you a pamphlet that is provided by the Heart Association that you can take home and share with your family."

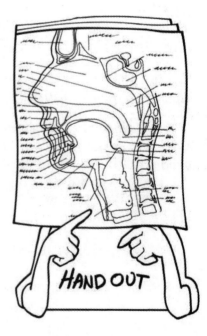

◎ Tell a personal story

One sure-fire way to win the approval of your audience is to tell a short story that demonstrates how you are personally involved with the topic. Keep your story short and to the point.

> *"Because I have allergies, I have had many sneezy, itchy experiences with my nose. Once I was even hospitalized. Despite these less-than-favorable experiences, I still think my nose is an amazing part of my body."*

◎ Thank your audience

This ending is simple but effective. It's always nice to thank your audience. Try using this technique along with other endings.

> *"This concludes my presentation on the amazing human nose. Thank you for listening."*

> *"I appreciate your attention. You've been a great audience."*

Chapter 4

Show Off With Visual Aids · · · · · · · · ·

A visual aid is anything you use during your report that your audience can look at while you are talking. There are lots of good reasons to use visual aids.

- ✔ Visual aids grab and hold the attention of your audience.
- ✔ Some people learn better by seeing information than by hearing it.
- ✔ Visual aids explain and reinforce what you are saying.
- ✔ Visual aids will remind you of what you want to say, so you won't have to look at your notes as often.
- ✔ Visual aids make your talk more fun to give and more fun to hear.

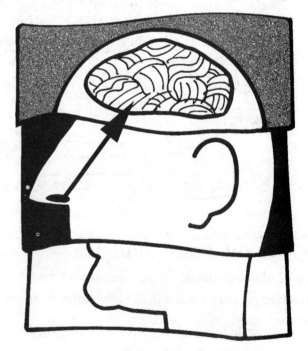

What you choose to talk about will give you ideas for visual aids. Try to make at least three visual aids for your topic. You can mix and match different types. Here are some visual aids that great speakers use.

☞ Posters and banners

These can be put up before your speech to make the class curious about your topic before you start. For "The Amazing Human Nose" report, you could hang a poster that shows the parts of the nose or a diagram of how information about scents is transferred from the nose to the brain. When you come to the part of your speech that your poster demonstrates, use a pencil or your finger to point to it.

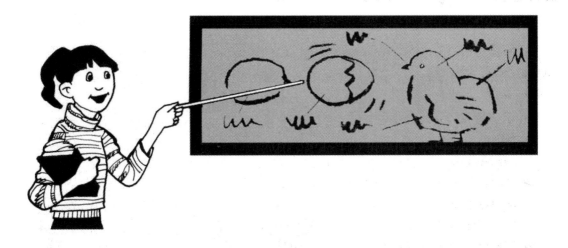

☞ Maps, time lines, diagrams and graphs

These visual aids can highlight your main points. They are best if you show them when you come to the part of your report that refers to them. One way to do this is to prop your map or graph on the chalkboard ledge, turned to the wall. When you come to the right place in your talk, turn it over and point to the information you want to show. You can leave it showing after you talk about it.

Another way to use maps, time lines, diagrams and graphs is to pass out a copy to each person in your audience. Pass out your visual aid before the speech and then ask people to refer to it at the appropriate time.

☞ Flip charts

Flip charts are big tablets of white paper on a cardboard back that you can find at most office supply stores. The paper is lightweight and easy to flip over. You might have several things you want to emphasize using a flip chart, so illustrations can be simple. For instance, the first chart might be a picture of a big nose as you introduce "The Amazing Human Nose." The second chart could list the four main parts of the nose, and the third chart could display a dollar bill with $100,000 written on it when you tell about "Da Schnozz."

Flipping the charts gives you something to do with your hands, and your pictures work like notes to help you remember what to say. Your audience will enjoy new visual aids for each part of your speech.

If you can see through the flip chart paper, staple or tape two sheets together at the bottom. Make arrangements with your teacher to display your flip chart on an easel or a tall chair.

☞ Chalkboards and dry erase boards

If you feel comfortable drawing or writing while you give your presentation, you can show your main points on the chalkboard or dry erase board. Practice what you plan to draw or write before your talk so you won't have to erase as you speak. Be sure to write legibly and large enough so it can be read by everyone in the room.

Get the teacher's permission to use the classroom boards and make sure there is enough empty board space and plenty of chalk. If you use a dry erase board, check the dry erase markers to make sure they work.

☞ Pictures from books

Pictures from books can be great illustrations of what you want to say, but if they are too small for people in the back of the room to see, you should make your own picture on a big chart or enlarge the picture. If you do use a picture from a book, practice walking around the room, up and down the aisles, showing the picture as you talk about it. Try not to use more than two book pictures during your report. Mark the page with a bookmark or paperclip so you can find it easily. Never tear or cut a picture out of a book.

☞ Passable objects and props

Props are objects you use in your report. For your report of "The Amazing Human Nose," you might use a model of a nose from the science department or samples of items with distinctive scents. Samples and souvenirs from home that are related to your topic make good props. In a report about early homesteaders, you could bring in your great grandmother's handmade quilt. At the close of a presentation on teaching dogs to do tricks, you could show off your cocker spaniel who can sit, roll over and shake hands. The props reinforce or illustrate what the speech is about.

You can show your prop or pass it around if it's not too fragile to be handled by everyone in your class. You should continue to talk while your prop is passed. If it will be too distracting for people to be passing a prop while they are trying to listen, show the prop and then arrange to put it on a table so people can look at it later.

☞ Costumes

Some reports are perfect for a costume. Dress up like the main character in your book report. Dress like a doctor if you're talking about first aid, like a soccer player if your topic is sports, or like a jester for a report on life in a Renaissance castle. Be sure you feel comfortable in your costume and will not feel self-conscious.

☞ Handouts and samples

Some reports lend themselves easily to samples and handouts. For a report on China, one student handed out a pair of chopsticks for everyone in the class. During a talk on Abraham Lincoln, the speaker gave out new pennies. After your presentation on Hawaii, you could distribute pineapple chunks on toothpicks.

Take a look at the information you've gathered, then use your imagination to come up with a good sample idea. Check with your teacher to be sure it's okay. You can display your samples while you talk, to create interest, or you can hide them until the end for a surprise.

Another kind of handout is a copy of something from your report. It might be a map of Rhode Island, a chart telling how to do the breast stroke, a graph showing eye color in America or a diagram of "The Amazing Human Nose." Let your report help you decide what information would be appropriate for a class handout.

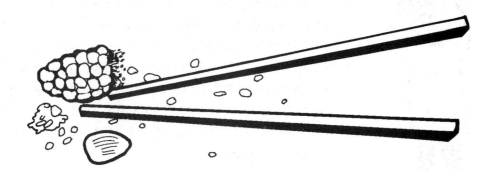

☞ Appealing to other senses

You can appeal to the senses of your audience either for real or by asking them to use their imaginations. If you bring in cinnamon and garlic to smell, a rabbit to feel, Idaho potato chips to taste, or a tape of Louis Armstrong to listen to, you have appealed to their real senses.

If you can't bring in the real thing or ask your listeners to close their eyes and use their imaginations to spark their senses. You can describe the sound of the waves lapping against the shore, the smell of salt in the air, the noisy din of Times Square on New Year's Eve, or the delicious taste of spices on a hot cheese pizza. An appeal to senses will reinforce your message.

☞ Use computer graphics

If your school has the equipment, you can put all the graphics for your speech on a computer that is attached to a projection system and project your visuals onto a screen. Your visual images can include a line-by-line outline of your speech or text that presents important facts. Interspersed with these facts should be pictures or graphics that will illustrate your text. This kind of presentation provides you with reminders of what you are talking about and also gives your audience pictures and graphics that are easy to view. It can be time-consuming to prepare the computer program, but it can also make a striking, memorable demonstration.

☞ Using aids effectively

Visual aids can highlight your presentation. They can demonstrate a point and make the subject come to life for the audience. They are effective in keeping the audience interested and involved. To make your visual aids the best they can be, remember these points:

☞ Make your visual aids big enough and clear enough to be seen clearly from the back row.

☞ Set up your visual aids before you begin. Make sure your visual aids are easy to reach and in the right order.

☞ Don't block your visual aid with your body. Stand to the side and gesture with your hand to call attention to the visual.

☞ Practice your presentation using the visual aids. Lots of practice will make you feel prepared and confident on the day of your speech.

Chapter 5
Pull Your Audience In! • • • • • • • • • • • •

It's fun to have the audience participate in your report. It keeps them interested and attentive and can make you feel more relaxed. There are several ways you can make your listeners active participants in your speech.

☀ Ask questions

An easy way to pull your audience in is to ask a question and call on people with their hands raised. If you like to use the chalk or dry erase board, write down answers or important information you want people to remember.

> *"Raise your hand if you have ever lived in another state. Which state, John?"*

> *"How many of you can name five different kinds of whales?"*

> *"What are some sports that are in the summer Olympic Games?"*

☀ Use a Survey

Another way to involve the class is to pass out a survey with questions related to your topic the day before your talk and then use the information in your report. Since your audience will have already had time to think about the questions and state their experiences or feelings, the information you present in your speech will be more personal to your listeners.

> *"Our classroom survey shows that only half of the people sitting in this room can roll their tongues."*

> *"My survey showed that everyone can identify the three largest states, but only four people knew what the fourth largest state is."*

☀ Give out a study sheet

Make up a study sheet with questions or blanks to fill in about the information you will cover in your talk. Ask the class to listen and fill in the answers as they hear them during your report.

1. The sense that is closest to taste is _____.
2. Jimmy Durante's nickname for his nose was_____.
3. The amazing human nose is made of _____, not bone.

Study sheets work best if the information you want the class to fill in goes in the same order as your talk. After your report, you can go over the study sheets together. This activity helps your audience review the information you presented and provides a nice ending.

☀ Give a quiz

Test yourself by testing your listeners. How much of your information did they really learn? How well did you hold their attention? Your quiz can be a show of hands or you can prepare a written quiz. Give the class a short amount of time, maybe three minutes, then go over the questions and answers together. Make it clear that this is a fun test, not a graded one. You can even include a humorous question or a question that requires a creative answer.

☀ Brainstorm

Brainstorming lets everyone participate. Ask a question (preferably an open-ended one that has many possible answers) and then write down any responses your classmates offer. Your goal is to get lots of answers, far-fetched as well as obvious. Ask questions like:

- In what ways can you ___?
- What are all the uses for ___?
- What are all the things that are ___?
- How many different ___ can you think of?

Start the discussion by suggesting one answer and writing it on the board. Add other answers to the list as they are contributed.

"How many uses are there for The Amazing Human Nose?"

✓ *Hold up glasses*
✓ *Show displeasure*
✓ *Smell when it's close to lunchtime*
✓ *Tell if milk is fresh or sour.*

Be ready to write fast on the chalk or dry erase board or ask someone to do it for you. Plan beforehand who will help you with the writing. After a short amount of time be ready to call a halt to the answers and move on with your speech.

☀ Make eye contact

The most important and effective way to pull your listeners in is to make eye contact with them. This will show them that you are talking to them personally, and that you care that they are listening. Try to make eye contact with people in every area of the room. This shows your audience that you are interested in all of them and in their reactions to your speech. This will also make you feel more relaxed.

Chapter 6

Speak Like a Pro · · · · · · · · · · · · · · · ·

After preparing an interesting talk, you want to deliver this information to your class like a pro. You want to sound calm, confident and organized. You want your audience to concentrate on the information you are giving them and not be distracted by your nervousness or mannerisms. Here are some ideas that will help you confidently deliver your speech.

☼ Use note cards

You can't make eye contact if you are reading your report from a sheet of note paper. Instead, you should use a note card to remind you of what to say. If you practice your talk and depend on your visual aids, you will be comfortable using note cards  instead of reading the speech word by word. Cards work better than paper because they are small, easy to handle, and they don't rattle or wrinkle.

One way to use note cards is in to put a main idea and a few points on each note card. You'll have a stack of cards, organized in the order of your presentation, to remind you of what to say. If you have a quotation or a list of facts you have trouble remembering, you can write them word-for-word on the cards, but mostly you will be telling your audience about your topic using only notes to remind you of the main points.

Another way to use note cards is to rehearse your speech enough that you can condense your reminder notes onto one card. One card is easier to handle than a stack of cards, especially if you need to put your notes down to present a visual aid. Use colors to highlight different notes so you can find what you need at a glance. A note card for "The Amazing Human Nose" might look like this:

Introduction - nose fact
Parts of a nose, visual 1
Nose functions, visual 2
How sickness affects noses
Life without smell
Pass cinnamon, garlic, visual 3
Closing - Hand out quiz, thank audience

☼ Practice your speech

The more you practice, the better your talk will be and the more confident you'll feel about giving it. Practice by yourself in front of a mirror. Practice for your family at home or ask a friend to listen to you. Ask someone to videotape your talk. The key to a smooth delivery is to practice, practice, practice.

☼ Add gestures and movements

As you begin to feel comfortable with your information and your visual aids, you will be able to add gestures that will enhance your words. For example, you might point to your own nose when you introduce your topic, "The Amazing Human Nose." The information in your report will guide you in choosing other gestures to fit your talk. Use gestures that add to your presentation and emphasize important information. Here are some gestures you might include:

☞ Open palms facing up when asking a question

☞ Pointing to the audience or to yourself

☞ Gesturing toward a visual aid

☞ A sweeping hand to include everyone in the room

☞ A fist to emphasize something you believe strongly

☞ Holding up fingers to illustrate a number

☼ Project your voice and smile

Practice speaking loudly and clearly. Without yelling, you want your voice to be loud enough to be heard throughout the room. If you are looking directly at your audience, your voice will be clearer. Slow down, take your time, and speak clearly.

Take a moment to pause and look at your audience. Give your audience a smile. You are prepared, your visual aids are great, and you have some important information to share. Look at your listeners and smile.

☼ Dress for success

On the day of your talk, wear something that is attractive but is also comfortable and won't be distracting to you or the audience. If you are worried or self-conscious about your clothes, you won't be able to concentrate on your talk. On the other hand, if your clothes are dirty, gaudy, or revealing, your listeners will spend more time studying your appearance than listening to your speech.

Chapter 7

Build Your Confidence • • • • • • • • • • •

Do you sometimes feel nervous in front of an audience? So does everybody else! This nervous feeling can actually make you do a better job because it gives you energy. Here are some ways to help you make the most of the butterflies in your stomach.

☑ Be prepared!

If you have prepared for your talk with lots of practice, good note cards, and exciting visual aids, you will do a super job. Make sure all your cards, props and visual aids are set up and ready to go before the time of your talk. Get to school early if you need to so you are not rushed. Know your talk, know your topic, and go in ready to impress your listeners with your fascinating information and smooth delivery.

☑ Practice!

Practice reciting your speech out loud many times. If you can, go to the room where you will be giving your talk when nobody is there. Stand where you will be standing when you give your speech to get the feel of being in front of the group. Go ahead and give part of your talk to the empty room. This will help you feel comfortable when the class is there.

☑ Think about your talk

When you make your presentation, give all your attention to the information you are telling the class. Don't think about yourself at all. Concentrate on explaining to the audience the great things you learned about your topic. Imagine yourself giving your talk clearly and with confidence. Visualize your talk just the way you want it to be. Think about what a success you'll be!

☑ Use your imagination

Use your imagination to visualize a situation that will make you feel in control and confident. You might try imagining your listeners are wearing their pajamas. If you imagine that everyone is wearing pajamas, it will help you remember that your listeners are just normal people like yourself. No reason to be nervous in front of people in PJ's!

You can make up other scenarios, too, if it helps you. Pretend you are the head of the FBI and you are giving a briefing to your special agents. Act like you are the world renowned expert in your field and you are speaking to a university group. Maybe you are a reporter on the evening news. Make up whatever scenario works for you and helps you feel self-assured.

☑ Breathe deeply or move around

Try a few jumping jacks or toe touches out in the hall before you begin. Even the act of walking to the front of the room can calm you. Use gestures when you talk. Moving puts that nervous energy to use. Take a few slow, deep breaths before you begin your talk. This will help relax you, too.

☑ Make eye contact

Before you begin, look your audience in the eye and smile at them. Take a moment to compose yourself and survey your audience. Remember, they are eager to hear what you have to tell them. Taking a second to look at them will relax you and put you in charge of the situation.

☑ Go through your preparation checklist

Go through your mental checklist before your talk. Even before you leave your seat and walk to the front of the room, think about whether you have your:

- ✓ notes
- ✓ visual aids
- ✓ handouts
- ✓ clean chalkboard
- ✓ anything else you might need

A quick mental inventory of what you have on hand to help you deliver your speech will reassure you that you are prepared and ready to deliver an extraordinary talk.

Chapter **8**

Branch Out - Specific Kinds of Reports

Most of the ideas in this book will work with any kind of talk. Often in school, however, the assignment will be for a speech on a particular subject. Here are some techniques for special kinds of reports that you may be assigned.

✸ Book Reports

Always tell the book's title and author at the beginning of your talk and bring in the book itself to display if you can. Try bringing in as many props from the book as you can think of and hold them up in order as you tell the plot of the book. This will help you remember what to say, give you something to do with your hands, and keep the audience listening and watching. Sometimes it is appropriate to dress as a character or show where the story takes place on a map.

✸ Biographical reports

Costumes are great for biographies. Try to dress like the famous person you're telling about. You can even give your talk from your subject's point of view. Props work well for biographies, too. One student who dressed like Betsy Ross sat in a rocking chair and sewed a flag while she told about Ross's life.

✹ Campaign speeches

Regardless of the office you're running for, your goal is to be remembered until voting time. There are many techniques that professional politicians use to get their messages to the voters. Many of these procedures can also be used to make your campaign speeches more memorable. Some ways to do this are:

☆ Have a catchy slogan that includes your name. Use it often. Rhymes, songs, and take-offs on popular commercials are easy for voters to remember.

☆ State why you should be elected clearly, simply and with confidence.

☆ Use any signs, banners or decorations that your school allows.

☆ Wear a costume or hat, but remember that you want to be taken seriously.

☆ Make eye contact and smile at your audience. Project your voice.

☆ If you need stage assistance, like holding up signs, consider asking people other than your best friends. This might show that other people support your candidacy and could possibly win you some extra votes.

☀ Science reports

Make a big impression by doing an experiment for the class instead of just telling about one, but be sure to practice first. Show your data on big colorful charts and use gestures to explain your research and what it means. If appropriate, show a model and explain how it works. Tell how this information affects people's lives.

☀ Geographical reports

Use a big map or globe to show the class the area you're reporting on. Try to dress like someone who lives there, either now or in the past. Bring a sample of the food from that area. Does the area have special music? Can you bring a recording of someone speaking in the native language? Show a replica of the state's or country's flag and explain the significance of its symbols.

Visual Aid Map

Poster Board

Chapter **9**
Conclusion · · · · · · · · · · · · · · · · · · ·

In room 5A, the teacher has just assigned an oral book report. Three students look nervous, one sinks down in his chair, and everybody groans.

* * * * * * * *

In room 5B, the teacher makes the same assignment. The students cheer and give high-fives, because they know how much fun it is to give oral reports and how much they can learn from listening to each other. They can't wait to make their outstanding, well-documented, interest-grabbing speeches.

My Speech

✎ **Possible topics**

_____

_____

_____

_____

Put a ★ by the topic you want to use.

✎ **Sources of Information**

_____

_____

_____

_____

_____

_____

_____

Take notes on other pieces of paper.

⇨ **Outline of information to be presented**

✏️ **Stories, facts, or jokes I could use**

_____

_____

_____

_____

_____

_____

✏️ **Ideas for an impressive closing**

_____

_____

_____

_____

_____

✏️ **Visual aids I could use**

_____

_____

_____

_____